Critique of Management Reason

Management Bits and Tips from Can't

Dmitry Vostokov

Published by OpenTask, Republic of Ireland

OpenTask books are available through booksellers and distributors worldwide. For further information or comments, send requests to press@opentask.com.

A CIP catalogue record for this book is available from the British Library.

ISBN-13: 978-1-906717-13-1 (Paperback)

Version 1.02 (January 2026)

Contents

I was supposed to publish this book in 2010 – an anthology of my people and project management posts from 2008 to 2010, when I was a manager and was roaming between management trainings. It started as a blog: Management Bits and Tips: Reflections on Software Engineering and Software Technical Support Management, which now survives as a Facebook page[1]. When I moved from management back to engineering, I wanted to publish a book with the original title, *Management Bits: An Anthology from Reductionist Manager*. Around 2015, I changed its title to *Critique of Management Reason: Management Bits and Tips from Can't* and added a few more bits as late as 2017.

---

[1] https://www.facebook.com/ManagementBits

Dmitry Vostokov is an internationally recognized expert, speaker, educator, scientist, inventor, and author. He founded the pattern-oriented software diagnostics, forensics, and prognostics discipline (Systematic Software Diagnostics) and Software Diagnostics and Observability Institute (DA+TA: DumpAnalysis.org + TraceAnalysis.org). Vostokov has also authored over 50 books on software diagnostics, anomaly detection and analysis, software and memory forensics, root cause analysis and problem solving, memory dump analysis, debugging, software trace and log analysis, reverse engineering, and malware analysis. He has over 30 years of experience in software architecture, design, development, and maintenance in various industries, including leadership, technical, and people management roles. Dmitry founded OpenTask Iterative and Incremental Publishing (OpenTask.com) and Software Diagnostics Technology and Services (former Memory Dump Analysis Services) PatternDiagnostics.com. In his spare time, he explores Software Narratology, Software Pathology, Software Morphology, Quantum Software Diagnostics, and Pattern-Oriented AI. His interest areas are theoretical software diagnostics and its mathematical and computer science foundations, application of formal logic, semiotics, artificial intelligence, machine learning, and data mining to diagnostics and anomaly detection, software diagnostics engineering and diagnostics-driven development, diagnostics workflow and interaction. Recent interest areas also include functional programming, cloud native computing, monitoring, observability, visualization, security, automation, applications of category theory to software diagnostics, development and big data, and diagnostics of artificial intelligence.

Management Bit and Tip 0x1

Flawless writing skills are very important to avoid a negative impression (bit). Use Google to check your writing (tip).

It is especially important for non-native English speakers like me. You can search simple sub-sentences and their alterations to compare search results.

For example, this sub-sentence: *"It's main advantage is "* gives **539** search results. However, the sentence without an apostrophe, "Its main advantage is ", gives **8,870** search results. Let's check combinations with two "it".

- "It's main advantage is it's " **192** results
- "Its main advantage is it's " **0** results
- "It's main advantage is its " **299** results
- "Its main advantage is its " **836** results

So, you get the idea of what is more correct or more widely used from a descriptive grammar point of view.

People feel uncomfortable if not irritated or alienated when they see their misspelled names (bit). Don't rely on your native language patterns or automatic spell checking. Verify names manually before hitting the "Send" button (tip).

For example, in English, it is rare when a person's name begins with both consonants, and it is harder to pronounce _Dm_itry or _Dm_itri (both are English and French spellings of the same Russian name) than _Dim_itry. Therefore, people tend to write the latter. Once, I got an email that started with "Dear Dirty". At that time, that was the default suggestion from Microsoft Word's spell checker.

Management Bit and Tip 0x4

Your boss needs a report, your boss's boss needs a report from your boss, your boss's boss's boss needs a report from your boss's boss, and so on, and everyone needs it before a certain date or even an hour. No one likes delayed reports, and no one likes writing them in a hurry (bit). Use the IIRW process, Iterative and Incremental Report Writing (tip).

People feel anxiety when the time approaches a deadline and reports are delayed. This affects both who needs to read a report and who needs to write it. So don't leave report writing to the last hour before the deadline to avoid delays. If you are in the software industry, you probably know about iterative and incremental software development. Apply it to report writing, too. Write reports incrementally as soon as you finish a task, subtask, or milestone, and revise them iteratively. This will also accommodate unexpected risks to report delivery when another boss is suddenly added to the middle of the reporting chain, requiring people below to shift their reporting time.

Day-to-day hands-on experience only is limiting (bit). Read books, articles, and blogs to deepen your understanding and broaden your knowledge, and then apply them to your day-to-day work (tip).

Sounds obvious, but so far, I have seen that engineers and managers en masse don't read or only read on a per-problem or per-task basis. It is a known fact that to really understand our subject matter, we need to read about other experiences, whether in science, engineering, or management. Even reading one book or article on a particular topic is not enough; it is better to read several to avoid bias and see different viewpoints. From my personal experience, I gained a much deeper understanding of C++ by reading many books. Although I applied hands-on C++ knowledge to a variety of projects, my real-world experience was very limited, despite writing and maintaining parts of a C++ compiler. For management roles, it is even more important to read, because managers cannot rely solely on day-to-day feedback. It might be too costly.

Past performance, success, and achievement records don't mean the same will hold in the future (bit). Look for the environment and hidden factors that explain the lucky side of success, and evaluate them in a new environment (tip).

The following book, which I vehemently recommend, influenced this bit and tip. Fooled by Randomness: The Hidden Role of Chance in Life and in the Markets. Although the book focuses on trading and material success, the ideas can be applied to hiring decisions and team building. Especially, contrary to the popular opinion that poor past performance persists, I've seen examples of poor past performance improving to above average, if not exceptional, after environmental changes. These changes don't mean leaving the company or pursuing an entrepreneurial career, but could involve changes within the same company. When hiring or promoting, I would also recommend considering the team's size. It is one case when there was a small team with two members and one star performer, and a completely different case when a team had 10 members with one star (clearly a Team Lead position). However, if a candidate was a star in 5 companies, but teams were 2-3 people in size, we clearly have the star performer against 10-15 people.

Management Bit and Tip 0x20

A full stomach affects clear thinking (bit). Avoid abruptly talking about work-related issues requiring thoughtful consideration and making decisions just after having a full lunch (tip).

Right after your lunch or near its end, you might lose control, start talking straight to someone, and use language that sends your message in the wrong direction, and you get the opposite result. I personally read science fiction and history books during my lunchtime and keep quiet. Keeping silence probably deserves its own management bit.

Management Bit and Tip 0x40

Management as a discipline has its own language (bit). Use language learning devices like dictionaries and practice, practice, practice business speaking and writing using every opportunity (tip).

What business management dictionary can I recommend for technical managers that covers the most frequently used phrases and terminology with the fewest number of pages possible, so that you can carry it with you? This one seems very good for beginners: *The Routledge Dictionary of Business Management*.

History and current affairs books are full of political case studies (bit). Read history books to get a balanced view of politics and better understand corporations, internal and external forces that shape them, and move people in, up, and out (tip).

I have loved history since childhood. I resumed reading history books after a long break as a software engineer. One of the books that I recently read is *The Naked Capitalist*. Reading this book prompted me to buy another one and start reading: *Tragedy & Hope: A History of the World in Our Time*.

Management Bit and Tip 0x100

Follow-up and Follow-through are essential skills of every manager (bit). In the absence of specialized software use your existing e-mail system to tag important e-mail messages with keywords (tip).

For example, when I send important analysis results, and I want to look at them in retrospect after a couple of months for postmortem analysis, I type the following tag at the end of my e-mail message: [*Dmitry Vostokov: revisit later*]

After some time, I just do a simple search in my inboxes to get all these tagged messages.

Management Bit and Tip 0x200

When receiving lots of e-mails, people pay attention first to something unusual (bit). Flag your request, inquiry, or FYI e-mail as low-priority when you send it to a general distribution list (tip).

Here you have a chance to get your e-mail noticed by curious people, and if you really sent something unimportant or inappropriate, you won't be accused because your e-mail was flagged as low priority.

Management Bit and Tip 0x400

Thick books impress people (bit). Write and publish a technical book related to your work to show the complexity and importance of what your team does and highlight the technical ability of your department (tip).

If others perceive the job of your team as easy and that tasks can be accomplished more quickly, a thick book shows the opposite and emphasizes quality over speed.

Management Bit and Tip 0x800

The pressure to deliver is great nowadays (bit). Utilize perennial time-proven software engineering techniques like reuse of accomplishments and artifacts (tip).

A classic example of this is called WORM: Write Once, Report Many. For example, you write an article once and report the number of views every month. Of course, the article needs to be popular enough to report.

Management Bit and Tip 0x1000

Some people don't feel good when they see themselves second or last on To: and Cc: email recipient lists or any other list that lists them (bit). Alphabetize the list and mention it casually (tip).

Prioritize, Alphabetize, Perspecti*wise*

The second P-word is not a misprint, but the summary that puts the alphabetization of To: and Cc: lists into perspective wisely!

From time to time, it is useful to have formal thank-you-for-your-service letters that emphasize how customers need your services for the day-to-day running of their business processes and/or during critical situations (bit). Have ready templates for asking about such letters (tip).

Follow through on prioritized service requests with feedback templates. If there are no critical issues, schedule periodical questionnaires. When people ask you for a service-favour, request a letter clarifying how your service-favour reply helped them to do their business.

Management Bit and Tip 0x4000

Many people don't want to accept help either personally or in an inter-team context (bit). Never suggest what you don't want for yourself, and even if you want help, suggest assistance (tip).

I originally learnt about this advice from Weinberg's book *Becoming a Technical Leader: An Organic Problem-Solving Approach*.

Management Bit and Tip 0x8000

In many companies, you can find various email and document retention policies that limit the lifespan of old reports in case you need them, for example, to compare your performance or defend your stance (bit). Use continuity in sending reports by replying to your previous report (tip).

This is actually an IIRW extension to bit and tip 0x4.

Management Bit and Tip 0x10000

It is impolite to attend a seminar, lecture, or training course and read a book there (bit). Use touch-style e-readers (but not Kindle, since it is too closely associated with books) to write notes, and switch to your favorite pages during breaks (tip).

In the past, I bought a Sony e-Reader PRS-600. Although its screen was a bit reflective compared to Kindle's, I liked its touch capabilities, especially when I needed to double-tap a word to see its definition in the dictionary quickly. Reflectiveness was usually not noticeable in the sunlight when I commuted. At home in the evening, when reflection was most evident, on a sofa, I preferred to read a real paper book.

Some people cling to their jobs, unwilling to move on, because of the potential redundancy payout they have accumulated over the years. They are just afraid of losing it when moving to a new job (bit). Consider job-hunting companies that offer a sign-on bonus. As a fraction of your possible redundancy package, it can ease your departure. Alternatively, divide your minimal redundancy package into the number of months, for example, the length of a probation period, and add this to the new compensation when negotiating with your potential employer (tip).

Management Bit and Tip 0x40000

Due to the complexity of the English language spelling and pronunciation rules, there will always be words you pronounce incorrectly unless you check every one in a pronunciation dictionary (bit). Consider running your text through a text-to-speech system as part of your preparation (tip).

I employed this technique as part of the preparation for the Webinar series on memory dump analysis.

Management Bit and Tip 0x80000

Some embarrassing spelling errors come from resulting semantic metaphors (bit). Develop a habit of checking the initial and last letters of typed words (tip). For example, *passthrough* and *look at your issue*.

Management Bit and Tip 0x100000

Sometimes you are asked to state or put down on paper what you feel, for example, during performance reviews (bit). If you want to avoid discussing the topic, politely reply with a smile that you are a machine that doesn't feel (tip).

Sometimes, it is good to be a machine.

A person or a company that makes a service request will feel a lack of attention to details and respect if you write a much shorter service response with less detail (bit). Spend, or at least show that you spent an equivalent amount of time and resources analyzing and answering a request. In some cases (technical support, for example) involving reciprocal request/response interactions, you can explicitly promise to spend the same amount of time if you request a time-consuming reproduction environment that helps you with troubleshooting or problem artifact analysis (tip).

Management Bit and Tip 0x400000

Research shows that employee productivity rises for the next 30 minutes after receiving a salary increase or a bonus (bit). Condition this timing for an employee to have the maximum impact (tip).

For example, in these 30 minutes, an employee may generate an idea that secures a company's future success or ensures that a project finishes on time with less budget.

Management Bit and Tip 0x800000

It's important to see signs of the approaching troubles from any possible angle, including social media like Facebook, LinkedIn, and Twitter (bit). For example, if your company or someone from the hierarchy above you follows you on Twitter, monitor that to catch the moment when that account stops following you (tip).

Management Bit and Tip 0x1000000

Some employees do not like their office space or complain privately when they are streamed, see "Downfloored or Upfloored?" (bit). If you happen to be one of them, justify this misfortune as having a free office (tip).

You can't get a nice office for free. Certainly, if you want to have a good office, you have to pay for it. Alternatively, employ the novel BYOOS method: Bring Your Own Office Space.

Management Bit and Tip 0x2000000

Some employees rush to connect on LinkedIn with as many colleagues as possible (bit). Don't rush; connect slowly from time to time to remind them of your existence (tip).

This is because new connections are visible in updates you remind about your existence, not only to a new *connectee*, but to all previously connected people.

Management Bit and Tip 0x4000000

Customer-facing skills are important (bit). What is equally important are Support Facing skills (tip). Support-facing skills are vital to get the best response from support and manage customer support expectations (what they expect from you, what you expect from them, you already know). One way to learn support-facing skills in a relatively mild way is to purchase your company's product while you are still employed (especially in support).

Management Bit and Tip 0x8000000

Modern corporate environments demand new forms of personal sacrifice (bit). Make the ultimate sacrifice by naming your child as your company name (tip). Examples: <Your Company Name>ina, <Your Company Name>in, <Your Company Name>a with generic catchalls Companin and Companina.

Management Bit and Tip 0x10000000

After a certain YS milestone (see YS Milestones), you may need to plan for future career progression, possibilities, and opportunities (bit). In such a case, set yourself a company standard probation period after which you decide on further steps (tip).

In the press and news, *forgiveness* was marked as one of the most important personality traits for leaders (bit). Don't forget that forgiveness is bidirectional: for people who work for you and for people you work for (tip).

With age comes aphorisms.

- "Empty office is the best office."
- "Two minds are better than one... if each one has a separate activity."
- "Think globally. Get paycheck locally."
- "Business is cold. The colder it is, the more superconductivity you have."
- "In politics, it is better to appear as if you have a short memory."
- "80% of energy is spent to get 20% of income."
- "If you leave a company, leave a front door open and rear windows clean."
- "Be clockwise. Always look forward. Don't be counter-clockwise."
- "The best products of a company are its people."
- "A job is like a critical section: you must leave after you enter."

```
EnterCriticalSection(&Job);
// ... do your job
LeaveCriticalSection(&Job);
```

Introduction

There is something similar, at least metaphorically, between computer system crashes and hangs and software project failures. Software projects deliver software that crashes, and these software failures, via a negative feedback loop, either slow projects down or simply lead to their abandonment. The structure of a software development team resembles that of a running application (called a process), with team members acting in parallel (threads), and the structure of an operating system, with multiple running processes competing for resources, resembles a software company struggling to stay alive. When projects fail, artifacts remain for study, and the same is true for crashed processes or operating systems, leaving crash memory dumps for postmortem analysis. Below are selected mappings

of Crash Dump Analysis patterns[2] to Project Failure
Analysis patterns.

---

[2] https://www.DumpAnalysis.org

Part 1

Recall from my motivation for this pattern series, the analogy between the following entities:

- Computer Application/Process – Team
- Thread of activity – Team member
- Operating system – Company organization and management
- Computer system – Company organization and management, plus teams
- User process dump – Team state snapshot
- Kernel memory dump – Organization state snapshot
- Complete memory dump – Organization state plus teams' internal state snapshot
- Exception – Fault, mistake
- Crash or hang – Failure

The first pattern, called Multiple Faults, is a direct mapping of the application crash analysis

Multiple Exceptions pattern[3]. The running instance of a computer application (process) can experience multiple exceptions from different execution threads before it hangs or crashes. The latter causes the process to disappear from external observers watching Task Manager. The same can be true for any functional team. Multiple faults from different team members can occur, and if a team fails, we shouldn't attribute the overall failure to just one member's fault that's on the surface; we should also look for other possible mistakes.

---

[3] Memory Dump Analysis Anthology, Volume 1
http://www.dumpanalysis.org/Memory+Dump+Analysis+Anthology+Volume+1

Part 2

What is the equivalent of computer memory in organizations and teams? It is a collection of various artifacts, including project documentation, source code, financial documents, etc. What is computer memory corruption? It is a deviation from expected memory contents that may or may not lead to a crash or a hang, but the chances of that are increasing over time. Metaphorically, we can consider deviations from requirements or expected documentation content to be a form of corruption that may slowly lead to a project's failure over time. Surely, "project memory" or "organization memory" is dynamic or heap-like in nature, as documents are added to a pile or removed from it. Therefore, we have just established the mapping between the Dynamic Memory Corruption pattern[4]

---

[4] Ibid.

from the crash dump analysis domain to the Project Artifact Corruption pattern.

Part 3

Metaphorical mapping from the False Positive Dump pattern[5] leads to the False Project Failure pattern, which usually occurs when assessing the current project status results in overestimating its potential failure, leading stakeholders to think the actual failure has already happened. Let me bring an example from my own software engineering experience. One of the software developers was assigned a project to develop a wizard-like installation system tightly integrated with voice recognition. For some reasons I don't want to discuss here, the system wasn't developed, and we faced a demonstration of it in front of the VP the next day, when we learnt that there wasn't even a prototype. However, that was only potential failure not turned into an actual one because we managed to create a working prototype overnight by typing screen dialogs in MS Word, printing them to

---

[5] Ibid.

bitmap files, drawing Next and Prev buttons in MS Paint, and crafting a small GUI program that sequentially displayed these pictures based on whether mouse clicks were in the region of painted buttons. The prototype was working like a clock, and VP was so impressed that he didn't even have any questions to ask. The project was abandoned in another 6 months, but this is another story and a different pattern.

Software Industrial Language

We can't use "Industrial Language" in software factories. But we can use debugging and troubleshooting vocabulary:

- Crash
- Hang
- Breakpoint
- Throw
- Exception
- Delete (this might be offensive to software-averse managers)
- Kill
- Suspend
- Trace
- Dump
- Leak

Science Fiction and Management

Part 1

I read a short SF story, *Stable Strategies for Middle Management* (by Eileen Gunn). The narrative is set in the future, where corporations use bioengineering to evolve employees into useful corporate organisms, such as insects. Some employees subscribe to evolutionary modifications to get ahead in their careers.

Now, when I'm reading SF novels or stories, I pay attention to management issues and come back with more parts and recommendations for this topic.

Part 2

The next recommended short SF story is *The Best We Can* (by Carrie Vaughn). Management disaster when an alien artifact is discovered in the Solar System. Poignant tale of fighting ideas and aspirations without management support. I imagine a continuation of that story: the alien artifact leaves the Solar System while management spends years in meetings. Once again, a civilization encounter is missed.

Management Poetics

Part 1

Management Poetics studies the theory of management literary forms and their literary criticisms. Consider this verse:

Four activities a day
Keep redundancy away.

What activities did the author mean? Was it a Quadrivium of reading, writing, speaking, and listening?

Part 2

When you are alone in a company and uncertain in your fate (career), it is better to refer to some great poetry and poets for consolation. My favorite is *No one listens to me... I am alone*, by the great Russian poet Lermontov[6]. You can find out the translation and its original Russian equivalent here: *I am alone* (Lermontov/Smirnov)[7].

---

[6] http://en.wikipedia.org/wiki/Mikhail_Lermontov

[7]

http://wikilivres.ru/No_one_listens_to_me%E2%80%A6_I_am_alone_(Lermontov/Smirnov)

Management Philosophy

Management Dialectics

Can and Can't: a struggle for a new synthesis.

Management: Analysis and Synthesis

I originally created the *Management Bits and Tips* category on my Crash Dump Analysis blog[8] to write my thoughts on management. Then I realized how this category title is metaphorically similar to the scientific modeling approach:

Analysis (Bits) -> Synthesis (Tips)

There are books and blogs with pure "analytic" titles:

- *Management Bits*
- *Management Bytes*
- *Management Bits and Bytes*

or with pure "synthetic" titles like *Management Tips*.

---

[8] www.DumpAnalysis.org/blog

I was thinking about the "Management QWords" category, but abandoned that thought because "QWord" sounds to me like an abbreviation for "Cursing Words". *Management DWords*? DWORD is an abbreviation for the computer memory term "Double Word," but it doesn't sound good from a management perspective. And, *Management Words* sounds like a dictionary title.

Heidegger at Work

This is an attempt to understand the world of work through the reading of the major works of Martin Heidegger[9]. We start with our interpretation of the basic ideas from his major work, *Being and Time*[10].

First, we say that a human being and a company are inseparable. There is a being-in-the-company that we call DasFirma. DasFirma is an existential mode of an employee being, who is fully aware that they are in the company doing a factual job. A being was thrown into a company and lost authenticity, becoming inauthentic. DasFirma is always projecting itself into a world of possibilities where job termination is an unavoidable event horizon. The life of DasFirma is shared with other DasFirmas by being alongside them. Other DasFirmas constitute an average field that DasFirma fell into. An average inauthentic

---

[9] http://en.wikipedia.org/wiki/Martin_Heidegger
[10] http://en.wikipedia.org/wiki/Being_and_Time

DasFirma forgets about termination (or redundancy) while being-in-the-company-towards-something. The glimpses of authenticity only happen when DasFirma expresses his mood. The source of any free time is in the future because DasFirma is always thrown into situations it didn't choose.

We continue to explore philosophical thought in the context of a job. Here, we provide an interpretation of what is usually called Hegelian dialectic, but was introduced by Fichte: thesis, antithesis, and synthesis[11]. In the context of job sequences, we have: employment, unemployment, and employment again. The second employment here is a double negation of the first employment, and so on up the ladder to the absolute job.

---

[11] https://en.wikipedia.org/wiki/Thesis,_antithesis,_synthesis

Existential Meaning of Endorsements

Its meaning is to remind your connectees about your existence. Management bit 0x2000000 already provided a tip about the velocity of reminders, so don't do all your endorsements at once. Also, don't do one endorsement per person, as it would ruin your reputation for generosity. Be moderate in endorsements.

Preemptive Multireading

Many people ask me how I manage to read all the books that I have. The trick is to employ Preemptive Multireading, similar to the so-called preemptive multitasking[12], using natural interrupt mechanisms. Here is an example from one of my common daily reading schedules:

- Commuting to work from home in the morning: reading a history book.
- Working hours: round robin reading of software engineering books and encyclopedias during breaks.
- Lunch time: reading one of the selected fiction/science fiction/health/food/chemistry/popular science books.

---

[12] http://en.wikipedia.org/wiki/Preemptive_multitasking

- Commuting to home from work in the evening: reading a selected math/physics/popular science book.
- Waiting for bus/train: one of the selected philosophy/popular science books.
- Home: one of the selected management/psychology/parenting books.
- Walking with my sleeping son on weekends: English language and writing books.

Cooperative Multireading

Although I still use Preemptive Multireading throughout my working day, I decided to try an approach similar to cooperative multitasking used in old operating systems like Windows 3.x. I identified 30 technical books I want to read (mostly related to software engineering, software architecture, design, and programming) and allocated 1 hour a day, spending about 2 minutes on each book. Most software-related books have low information density per page, and much of the information is repeated from book to book, which allows the use of some speed-reading techniques. These books are unlike mathematics, physics, and computer science books, where I have to meditate on proofs, formulae, and examples. So I switch to another book every 2 minutes and do this 30 times. 2 minutes is usually sufficient to read and turn a page, and this amounts to 60 pages per day (one page per minute). An average 300-page book can be finished in 7-8 months, so I can read at least 30 books per year using this approach, read all of them together, and not wait for a second book until I finish the first one! The last point is psychologically very important to me because I want everything now.

A technical note: it might look like we still use preemptive multitasking with a fixed quantum here, but in reality, there are no external interrupt sources. All I do is voluntarily yield reading control from one book to another. I can always spend one or two minutes more with a book if its current chapter is very interesting.

Strategic and Tactical Personal Learning

Some people learn strategically to enhance their skills horizontally in a hiring landscape. When hired, they assess what is common knowledge and skills in the given industry or industry segment. A typical example is mastering C++ programming and its features up to the C++ standard. Another example is learning Windows internals to enhance debugging skills if the company develops Windows software. Sometimes strategic learning stems from a desire to gain deep insights or to become a better contractor or technology expert. Other people learn tactically, for example, the hiring company's product internals. Some people take a balanced approach. Some do not learn anything, for example, Process Parasites.

Physics and Mathematics for Managers

Digitizing a Manager

As you might have noticed, I have already described the essential management bits that form part of a management bit vector[13]. For example, 0110... bit vector describes a manager who:

- writes with mistakes (0x1)
- never misspells names (0x2)
- writes reports on time (0x4)
- doesn't read management books (0x8)
- ... (0x10)
- ... (0x20)
- ...

---

[13] Looking with hindsight in 2025, I was doing the so-called feature engineering.
https://en.wikipedia.org/wiki/Feature_engineering

So, you can digitize any manager using management bits as observables. This sounds like a reductionist approach to life sciences, but at least it is manageable. You can also digitize any employee or job candidate to form their employee bit vector or candidate bit vector and see how their bit vectors are close to your acceptable bit mask or even your own bit vector, and this can be the basis for a promotional assessment or hiring decision.

Also, you can see that 32 essential management bits yield 4 billion distinct managers. To cope with this combinatorial explosion, we might need to introduce management subsets or management bitmasks.

Have you ever felt doubt when assigning or distributing "meets some", "meets all", or "exceeds performance" ratings across your team members when delivering feedback during performance appraisals? This is the problem for high-performance team leads who are promoted to management positions. They compare other team members to their past performance and feel that all fall under the "meets all" category at best. However, they should calculate the mean performance indicators and rate team members based on that mean. For example, your team members had the goal of writing knowledge base articles (without specifying a predefined number). Sure, when you were the team lead, you wrote 20 of them during one night. That's why you were promoted. Now you see that Adam wrote 1, Sophie wrote 3, and John wrote 5. Hmm, they all look underperforming for you. However, this team without you as an engineer is the new team. So, calculate the mean : (1 + 3 + 5)/3 = 3. Therefore, it would be fair to say that Adam "meets some", Sophie "meets all", and John "exceeds performance".

Twin Employee Paradox: Special and General Relativity of Career

It is a known fact of special relativity that "the faster you move, the more slowly you age."[14] But it has been known for thousands of years that the faster you move up the career ladder, the slower you age; the slower you move up the career ladder, the faster you age. However, the career space is not simply connected; it is riddled with topological breaks: the faster you move down the career ladder, the faster you age. This was confirmed numerous times when people aged overnight after being demoted.

---

[14] The Philosophy of Physics, by Dean Rickles

Set Theory for Managers

A conversation between a manager and a mathematically inclined engineer:

M. Do you have an opinion about this project?
E. Yes, I have a unique set of positive opinions.
M. Tell me.
E. It's an empty set.
M. You lied to me!
E. No, an empty set is still a set, and it is unique[15].

––––––––––––––––––––––––––

[15] https://en.wikipedia.org/wiki/Empty_set

Luck-Lines: Special and General Relativity of Success

You can't catch luck until you meet it at some point in space-time. No matter how hard you try to follow luck, you won't be able to catch it until your line intersects a luck-line. Luck is always faster than you. This is the essence of Special Relativity of Success. Luck-lines may be attracted and then bent by curved space-time. Such luck-gravitational anomalies usually result in earlier intersection with luck-lines (the so-called fast-tracks). Those who can manipulate indices of the Rich-tensor can better predict various intersections. This is the essence of General Relativity of Success.

How to Spot Statistics Talent

If you need an employee with a statistical bent, ask appropriate questions during the interview, for example: "What would you do if you came to a cafeteria and found that you needed to empty a coffee machine bin?" The word *bin* should trigger an appropriate answer after the appropriate counter questions (coffee machines vary), for example: "I would count the distribution of various coffee pack types in the bin".

Classical and Quantum Mechanical Employees

A classical employee.

When a manager measures an employee's position and momentum, they are found to be precise and consistent with expectations.

A QM employee.

When a manager makes a measurement, he or she finds either a position or momentum, but not both.

LAMB: Laboratory of Abnormal Management Behavior

In addition to Project Failure Analysis Patterns (PFAP) and to facilitate further research on patterns, we opened a laboratory to study patterns of abnormal management behaviour and their diagnostics. Managers are watched, measured, and analysed behind their backs to minimize observer interference. I would also suggest that measured managers not measure an observer, because a destructive resonance may occur, similar to the Activity Resonance pattern[16] in software diagnostics (which has an equivalent in management when 2 managers try to manage the same team or project independently). The research director of the laboratory was chosen for his experience in both insider and outsider management.

---

[16] Memory Dump Analysis Anthology, Volume 7
https://www.dumpanalysis.org/Memory+Dump+Analysis+Anth
ology+Volume+7

PS. A personal note: dishes from lamb are one of my favorites in Ireland. When I'm in a restaurant, I first look for lamb (and duck).

Thermodynamics of Career

Reading some posts about becoming-a-manager led me to introduce the notion of "Career Thermodynamics" using physical thermodynamics as a metaphor. For example, the local concentration of some features becomes equalized with the system when an individual is put on a career path, and the system does some work on that individual.

Promotional Waves Detected

Finally, our LAMB (Laboratory of Abnormal Management Behaviour) detected the primordial promotional waves through a delicate Lamb shift experiment. They originate from A New Employee Big Bang inflationary period (some call it a probation period). They travel ahead of an employee's path, but physical people around fail to notice them until they hit unexpectedly hard. Some man agement (see Man Agement Aphorisms) theories of an earlier company universe formation say they are of a *Plan*'x length quantized by quarters.

Another Meaning of NDA

You hear there, "I work under NDA," and you are not given any details. Use the principle of least action [17] borrowed from physics to provide a stationary explanation: NDA means Not Doing Anything.

- What do you do there?

- NDA.

---

[17] http://en.wikipedia.org/wiki/Principle_of_least_action

YS Milestones

YS (Years of Service, pronounced as *wise*) can be classified according to base numbers:

- B grade (2 YS)
- O grade (8 YS)
- D grade (10 YS)
- H grade (16 YS)

Downfloored or Upfloored?

Downflooring/upflooring could be the mild version of downsizing, promotion, or demotion, depending on the office space plans for your next office move. It could also mean nothing if staff streaming is rotational, as mathematicians say, div rot S = 0, or it might indicate which employee team or functional unit is important if streaming was done relative to a non-movable office. It might also mean team compression, to minimize staff gradient, as mathematicians say, grad T = 0.

A Guide to Corporate Canteens

> *Tell me what your canteen is,*
> *and I will tell you what your company is.*

During my rare visits to Irish pubs, I sometimes meet people who work or have worked in the same companies I previously worked for. While recalling past times over a few beers, I always mention the canteen experience. A few weeks ago, when I introduced myself as a writer, I was told it would be great to start writing a book about corporate canteens similar to popular guides to pubs, bars, and restaurants. And I was even immediately invited to a corporate canteen for a starter!

So, let's begin with a canteen I visited ten years ago (2000) in Moscow, Russia. The company I worked for at that time was Luxoft, a part of the bigger IBS Group Holding. As we were sitting in an office recreated from a former factory, we had to go to lunch at another building where the IBS headquarters were located. The food was good but expensive (not subsidized), and sometimes, as part of the team building exercise, we were also walking to another nearby canteen that belonged to some scientific institute, I don't recall the name of. The good thing about the IBS corporate canteen was that we occasionally saw top Russian corporate and IT strategists. If they were eating there, the food must be really good. I still remember some dishes despite their small portioned size. Salads were traditionally Russian. Sometimes there were even free tables where you could sit and eat in solitude. At that time, I didn't think of reading a book during lunchtime. I also noticed cognac was available for purchase separately. However, I don't recall seeing employees drinking spirits in that canteen. We could even walk after lunch, as there were quiet places outside with benches and trees. However, I had never come to that idea at that time.

The Rise in Interest in Corporate Canteens

Google Analytics was collecting stats for "canteen" search keywords that led to the originally published article on the former blog:

- corporate canteen guide
- corporate canteen
- "corporate canteens" analysis
- a good corporate canteen
- canteen etiquette
- canteen tips
- canteens in corporate
- corporate canteen contract
- corporate canteen etiquette
- corporate canteen names
- corporate canteens
- examples of the best on-site corporate canteens
- a few words about corporate canteens
- managing canteen tips
- tips for a good canteen

- tips on how to start a canteen
- working of the canteen in the organization

Q&~A: BIQ Questions

We propose Baffle Interviewer Questions. These are questions to end the odd interview or just to show off how you are out of the box. However, as History teaches us, what is abnormal today may be perfectly normal tomorrow. So the first few questions are about GMOs in the office.

- Does food in your canteen contain GMOs?
- Is your corporate coffee GMO-free?
- Do you do business with GMO companies?

You may not get an answer to your questions. This is why we use the symbol of negation from formal logic ~ in Q&~A. Or you may get hints from an interviewer: Did you mean *that* GMO? So this prompts further BIQ questions.

Book Proposals

Definitely, there is a shortage of some management and work-related books. When a topic is negative, there is a shortage of positive, and vice versa. When there is a critical book, there is no corrective book. Here, I try to diagnose such deficiencies and provide recommendations. For example, there is a book, *English with an Accent: Language, Ideology and Discrimination in the United States, Second Edition*. But there are no career-enhancement books like *Learn Your Boss Accent in 21 Days* (or 24 hours). Of course, there are accent-improvement books and training courses, but we need a book focused on the right words, spoken with the right accent.

Book Review: Managing Humans

I read this interesting non-mechanical book on people management written by Michael Lopp, *Managing Humans: Biting and Humorous Tales of a Software Engineering Manager*. I borrowed the term "mechanical" manager from him to describe his book as non-mechanical. The second chapter, "Managers are no Evil," is worth reading alone as it provides a simple answer to a venerable question asked by engineers: "What does my manager do?" The stories in this book come from software engineering companies ranging from startups to big ones. Highly recommended for technical support engineers and team leaders promoted to management positions to get insight into their new role, avoid mistakes, and prevent blow-ups.

Missing Chapters from Management Books

I found the book Selling the *Work Ethic: From Puritan Pulpit to Corporate PR* in a local library and was intrigued by its title and table of contents. After reading it from cover to cover, I must say I was really surprised to learn much more about capitalism and the unfolding of consumer society than I learnt during the Soviet era from Marxist propaganda. Having a big management library myself, I would say I never questioned why all these management books were printed. To know why you need to read this book. Funny enough, after reading, I stumbled across a demo of a computer game about SpongeBob where he was working hard and was about to be promoted to a management position. While walking around his house, he met a welfare creature who asked him not to forget him after his promotion. The whole episode now looks from a fresh "selling work ethic" perspective, especially after I learnt that the CD came from a packet of children's food bought in Tesco (selling work values to kids?). I liked the book and bought another one from the same author, *This Little Kiddy Went to Market: The Corporate Assault on Children*, and a biography, *Benjamin Franklin: An American Life*.

Fine Collection of Management Antipatterns

To my shame, I have never read the famous book *AntiPatterns: Refactoring Software, Architectures, and Projects in Crisis*. Being interested in antipatterns, which I often figure out myself in the practical domain of software technical support (see Crash Dump Analysis AntiPatterns in my anthology volumes[18]), I looked for the most recent collection of management ones. I found this book, which I'm reading now: *Antipatterns: Identification, Refactoring, and Management*.

In addition to their own patterns, the authors of the book describe Brown's antipatterns (the book mentioned earlier, *AntiPatterns: Refactoring Software, ...*), provide two tables for easy antipattern identification in an organization or team: (Management Antipattern Locator, Environmental

---

[18] https://www.dumpanalysis.org/advanced-software-debugging-reference

Antipattern Locator), list and comment on Myers-Briggs personality types, discuss Keirsey temperament groupings and Bramson's human personality phenotypes. Highly recommended. I especially liked the "All You Have Is a Hammer" antipattern, which I was guilty of myself during my earlier Team Lead role.

Expectations, Expectations...

I found this book in a local bookshop, and now I recommend it to everyone dealing with customers, either internal or external: *Managing Expectations: Working with People Who Want More, Better, Faster, Sooner, NOW!* for which Gerald Weinberg wrote the foreword.

Bullshit Bibliophilia

I own a few books about bullshit, and reading them is great fun. The first one is about bullshit in economics, politics, medicine, marketing, sales, and many other areas of human activity. I read it completely two years ago and highly recommend: *The Dictionary of Bullshit*.

The second book is very short, easy to carry around, and looks like Tractatus Bullshito-Philosophicus: *On Bullshit*.

The last two books, and the first of them is the dictionary that seems to be very funny too: The *Dictionary of Corporate Bullshit: An A to Z Lexicon of Empty, Enraging, and Just Plain Stupid Office Talk*. The other one seems to be a compilation of various philosophical works with guaranteed results: *Bullshit and Philosophy*.

A Thread Was Killed

The title of this post employs an operating system metaphor for a team member as a thread in a process (team). I recalled a book I had read years ago and dug it out from one of my dark, dusty office corners: *My Job Went to India: 52 Ways to Save Your Job (Pragmatic Programmers)*.

I think it is relevant in any economic downturn if you replace India as an empty set or empty string: My Job Went to "".

Hidden Transcripts

"... those people who are really good at what they do and yet are at the bottom of a management hierarchy have a power that no one else in the hierarchy has. They can't be demoted. "

Robert Glass, *Facts and Fallacies of Software Engineering*

Understanding and overcoming resistance is a manager's task. A public performance (transcript) of the manager is different from an inner transcript, and the same can be said about transcripts of engineers. I now recall that, in one of the previous companies I worked for, a senior engineer told a recently hired junior colleague in a private setting (the canteen) to always tell the VP of Engineering how much he loves the work. I recently became interested in the analysis of managerial domination, various forms of hidden resistance, the stage performances of subordinates, and the internal pressures they experience. Doing my research, I stumbled across this book: *Domination and the Arts of Resistance: Hidden Transcripts*.

The book is written in an almost jargon-free style. It is highly recommended as a stimulating and refreshing read that offers additional perspectives on relations within teams and engineering organizations, and between customers and their relationship managers (inverse domination).

If you move to work in another country, it is always useful to read about local workplace norms, redundancy regulations, various employment acts, and other smart knowledge. If you happen to be a native of that country, then you should prefer to read such books as well. More than 8 years ago, when I moved to work in Ireland, I bought this guide (one of the previous editions): *Working and Living in Ireland*.

Years later, I was visiting a local bookshop and browsing the bargain section, where I found *Smart Moves at Work in Ireland* by the same author and immediately bought it. The "Exit" chapter is recommended to read during the current turbulent times in the Irish economy.

The Science of Career Promotions

In a local Dun Laoghaire bookstore, I stumbled upon this book: *Who Gets Promoted, Who Doesn't and Why: 10 Things You'd Better Do If You Want to Get Ahead*.

Initially, I hesitated, but finally bought it. I wasn't disappointed when I started reading it that evening. This book finally provides an explanatory framework for career promotions, and it really fits well with my observations from the companies I worked for over the years. This book also teaches some important vocabulary, such as:

- future value;
- a smooth handoff within the window of opportunity;
- optimization of the outcome of the staffing change.

Two Faces of Mess and Management

Isn't it that management is about creating organization from a mess (chaos)? In other words, good managers thrive on mess. Isn't it that management is about preventing mess from appearing in an organization? In other words, management is about the complete annihilation of mess. This is what I thought until one day, when in a local book store, I found this interesting book, was intrigued by its title, and bought it: *A Perfect Mess: The Hidden Benefits of Disorder–How Crammed Closets, Cluttered Offices, and On-the-Fly Planning Make the World a Better Place.*

I believe from an evolutionary perspective, mess provides sources of randomization necessary for survival and fitness of the organization. If we are self-organizing ourselves, then how do we know that we have chosen the best structure and strategy? If we believe we are right, aren't we ultimately *Fooled by Randomness*?

Sabotage Studies

It is a fearful word everyone now avoids, but every manager needs to study it. Once, I visited a used books shop that was about to close in Dun Laoghaire (Dublin, Ireland). There was an influx of books on Marxism and the Labor Movement in 1950-1980. While glancing at book spines, I noticed this title: *Sabotage: A Study in Industrial Conflict* by Geoff Brown. Published in 1977. Signed by Manuel.

I bought it for 3 euros. Interesting title. It even has a chapter on Stakhanovism[19].

---

[19] https://en.wikipedia.org/wiki/Stakhanovite_movement

Reflecting on my old software engineering days, I remember working for one of the biggest software factories in Russia and noticing Internet Explorer windows on workstations as I passed by. Then, working for one of the biggest software factories in the telecommunications domain, I noticed the same screens whenever I entered the engineering offices. People there obviously had plenty of time for browsing, reading, and typing (not in some programming language, of course). At that time, I started calling them Process Parasites and their relationship to a team and an organization as Process Parasitism, which (paraphrasing Wikipedia definition[20]) is:

---

[20] http://en.wikipedia.org/wiki/Parasite

A type of symbiotic relationship between an employee and an organization in which one, the process parasite, benefits from a prolonged, close association with the processes in the organization.

What kind of benefits does a process parasite gain? Obviously, one benefit is time: free time to do whatever a parasite wants or needs, but irrelevant to business goals. This especially happens when there are process inefficiencies and insufficient resource planning.

One manager reading this post noticed the curious similarity between the word "web<u>site</u>" and the word "para<u>site.</u>"

Contributing Process Parasite

After reading biographies for some time, I decided to extend the notion of process parasites to the notion of a contributing process parasite. Let me give you an example. Recall that Einstein made his discoveries while working in a patent office where he had free time. Would the management of that office have tolerated it if they had known what he was doing while processing patent applications for clock devices? So, let's define a contributing process parasitism:

An extension of a process parasitism between an employee and an organization in which one, the process parasite, makes a contribution to humanity or to a specific domain of activity in general.

ECHO Stages of Corporate Citizenship

One of the outcomes of reading a book, *Comments on the Society of the Spectacle* (by Guy Debord), is the possible evolution of feelings of a corporate citizen, where the last stage corresponds to a spectator:

ECHO

Enthusiasm
Confusion
Hating
Onlooking

KAKA POPs: KAKA Principle of Power Shift

A colleague surprised me yesterday when telling me he was reading a book on power. I asked him why, and he told me he wanted to learn how to use power in his organization. Immediately, I seized an opportunity to lecture him on power basics because I also read a few books on power and had been digesting them for some time. So I told him the Principle of Power I discovered through sheer reading of case studies, mainly power struggles in communist Russia (POP, like a stack operation if you know a bit about computer science or programming). This was later generalized to POPs, the Principle of Power Shift:

Kiss Ass. Kick Ass.

Hope you find this succinct definition useful and easy to remember.

Note: The proper sequence is very important for your mental health.

Signs That You Have an Extraordinary Employee

1. Wrote several books.
2. Reads lots of books.
3. Has several blogs.
4. Founded a discipline.
5. Founded a company.
6. Published many ideas.
7. Has a lot of unpublished ideas.
8. Still an employee.

How to Talk About God in a Job Interview

You can mention god a few times and will not violate the separation of workplace and religion by simply using the word 'dog' as a test case for your string reversal algorithm, which you just designed and are currently explaining on a blackboard to an interviewer. The latter might even think that you are addressing the interviewer.

Management Programming Language

Let me introduce a new programming language. The name candidates were MPL, Man, and finally Ma. I choose the latter one as the root (cause) of all management. The first management operator is called an assignment. Its syntax is:

A <- B;

This assignment can be nested (delegated):

A <- B <- C <- D;

Remeritus Employee vs. Emeritus Remployee

The power of REM, the Visual Basic removal: either you are a *rem*eritus employee, paid but forgotten, or an emeritus *rem*ployee, remembered but not paid anymore, c'est la vie.

Working with software support artifacts such as memory dumps, traces, and logs (not even mentioning debugging) requires concentration, meditation, and total absorption to attain an enlightened understanding of the issue and then to communicate its solution and further recommendations clearly. This is why we are proposing this new set of practices. The name comes from Zen teaching and an Idle work ethic, where the latter is a combination of salaried employment and a small side business for a balanced life. If you have never encountered an idle alternative work ethic before, please check the wonderful *Idler* magazine[21].

---

[21] https://www.idler.co.uk/

Management and History

"He, like Napoleon, spent the end of his career in a small company."

Employee's Shelfie

An employee's bookshelf can be very revealing. Does it have a book recently recommended by top management? Are there only practical books, or are there some theoretical ones too? What books on topics other than job-related are there? Are they unmoved for extended periods, or permanently until employee streaming? Are there first editions only published ten years ago, or the most recent ones? Are they in a foreign language? Many questions can arise in the minds of those passing by. If you prefer having your bookshelf at home but don't want to look like a bookless employee, you can pin an enlarged picture of your home bookshelf at work.

More Than the Right Interview Answers

Q. Why did you leave a management position?

A. This is because I didn't want to lose my high creativity skill.

Difficult Choice: Engineering vs. Science vs. Management

Sometimes we face a difficult career decision or rationalize a previous one. Here's an ad I found that is a bit helpful (although I don't fully agree with it) while commuting one day. A Quiz: Which line on the badge is for engineering?

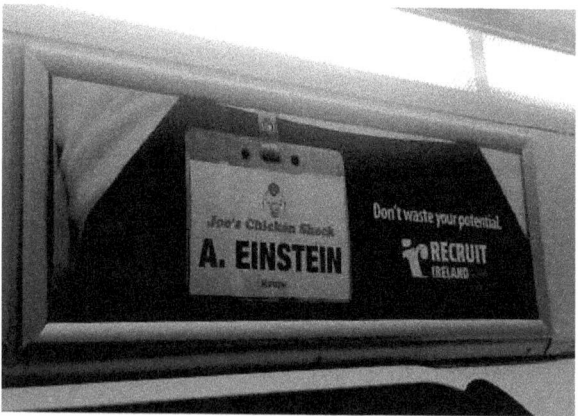

How to Get Ideas in the Office

Imagine an office space where books are on every corner and in every place, ready to be read. An employee opens a book, and ideas freely flow into his or her mind. Imagine another office where books are locked or absent. There are no ideas there: only a rehash of old ideas or ideas from competitors heard through press releases or ideas from customers. So, the moral is this: if you need fresh ideas, make physical books freely available to your employees.

Management Tyrants

Joseph Stalin used to say, when assigning goals to state employees, "No harm in trying." In Russian, this proverb is translated as "попытка не пытка" and has an additional connotation if translated literally: "A try isn't torture." This can be further extended to "A startup is not a permanent job."

Note: other translations:

"Nothing ventured, nothing gained."
(idiomatic/proverbial)
The most natural everyday equivalent is:
"It doesn't hurt to try."

In addition to the multitude of inspirational quotes circulating, we start with the first quote on persistence. It is called "The Day I Quit". Feel free to apply it to your job, hobby, relationship, etc.

∞

The Day I Quit

A Persistent Quote.
Copyright © 2014 by Dmitry Vostokov, DumpAnalysis.org

Another Meaning of ROFL

For some, it is ROFL; for others, it is "Redundancies On the Floor, Lying".

The Simplest Presentation Explained

I created the simplest presentation. You can download it from here[22]. Here's a slide-by-slide analysis for busy or download-averse readers. The zero slide names the presentation and its presenter. It also provides contact information.

The Simplest Presentation

Dmitry Vostokov

www.PatternDiagnostics.com

22

https://www.patterndiagnostics.com/files/TheSimplestPresentation.pdf

The first slide paints a black picture. The problem.

The second slide paints a white picture. The solution.

We Got a Reference

We are happy to see the original title of our book referenced in the article *Sherlock Holmes and the Adventure of the Rational Manager: Organizational Reason and its Discontents*[23]:

"Dmitry Vostokov (2010) called up the very notion of a reductionist manager to present the lessons he believes software design theory and practice can bring to understanding managerial problems."

---

[23]

https://www.academia.edu/6305420/Sherlock_Holmes_and_the_adventure_of_the_rational_manager_Organizational_reason_and_its_discontents_?sm=b

ERRoR: Employee Record Repository of Reports

We introduce Guinness World Records analog for the corporate world. It is called ERRoR. Employee Record Repository of Reports or Employee Report Repository of Records. Here, a record is not a database record but an achievement record. The idea came to us when we received a report about an employee who had never complained about office space for 42 years. Due to the nature of the corporate world and the accompanying NDAs, we have to anonymize the records upon receipt of the report.

OWE: Out-of-Warranty Employee

In addition to hardware and software, an employer needs to keep an eye on its wetware warranty either by upgrading (for example, with shares and perks) or replacing it with the new working units. We welcome the former and oppose the latter.

Employment Relationship: A Marital Analogy

A relation of an employee to an employer and vice versa can be metaphorically modeled by these stages:

Fiancée

Feelings of admiration and love from a potential employee towards an employer or from a potential employer towards a desperately needed future employee.

Married

Employment contract. After that, a relationship path can diverge into these states:

Separated

An untouchable or ignored employee or employer. No feelings or other ties other than basic bottom-line contractual obligations like monthly payments and office hours.

Divorced

When an employee is made redundant, dumped, or quits a company voluntarily.

Widowed

When one party or both are deceased.

The 48 Laws of Intellectual Power

Inspired by Robert Greene's book *The 48 Laws of Power*, I began carving my own laws of intellectual power. Sometimes they are direct opposites, like the first law:

Law 1

Always outshine the master.

Rationale

Make observers feel that you are superior. Impress them with your intellect. Go far in displaying your talents, or you accomplish the opposite: others will outshine you.

Signs of Overqualification

Observing people maturing in their profession, I found these signs of overqualification visible when a person:

- Becomes more proficient with foundational issues in contrast to specific minutiae.
- Spends more time on specific issues due to the accumulation of deep foundational knowledge in the respective discipline.
- Delivers less from the current job requirements, for example, an architect as a builder.
- Starts reading and thinking a lot.
- Publishes a seminal book.

Relativization of Stress

Stress can be relative. Instead of internalizing stress, an employee can stay calm and stress his or her environment. If everyone externalizes stress, then no one is under stress. This seems like a paradox – where has stress gone? The explanation is very simple: there was no stress initially!

On Management Amnesia

Have you ever been worried about managerial amnesia? There are two types: full amnesia and partial amnesia. The latter one is the most dangerous. Being selective, it provokes worries. Full amnesia, on the contrary, might stem from the current organization's focus on other functional areas and could even be confirmation of trust. Here is the story. I was made redundant in one company a long time ago. A month before that, I asked to replace a light bulb in the room because I used to work very long hours. However, the light bulb had never been changed, and only after redundancy did I realize it was one of the warning signs: there was no need to replace the light bulb – I was one in the office, and after my redundancy, the room became empty.

A definition:

A people manager who abdicates and becomes one of the former subordinates to increase customer satisfaction in crisis times when no headcount is available.

Flattening My Management

In 2009, I came back to an engineering role again after serving two years as a Team Lead and then almost two years as a Technical Manager[24].

So instead of growing vertically as a Manager, I decided to focus on horizontal growth because I also held additional management roles as Editor-in-Chief of Debugged! magazine[25], Founder and Editor-in-Chief of OpenTask iterative and incremental publisher [26], Founder of Software Diagnostics Institute[27]. At the same I needed to spend more time growing my technical knowledge and digging deeper into memory dumps.

---

[24] The Importance of Being Technical
https://www.dumpanalysis.org/blog/index.php/2009/04/10/the-importance-of-being-technical/
[25] http://www.dumpanalysis.org/Debugged+Magazine
[26] www.OpenTask.com
[27] www.DumpAnalysis.org

Rhetorical Question Disorder

Have you ever seen or worked with a person who never provides concrete answers, or in the worst case, doesn't answer at all? Perhaps this person considers any question as rhetorical[28] and therefore has RQD. You need to stop asking questions and make statements instead.

---

[28] http://en.wikipedia.org/wiki/Rhetorical_question

Managerial Stoicism

What is your philosophical and ethical foundation for all your managerial actions? I finally understood that mine is called Managerial Stoicism and is based on an old school of Hellenistic philosophy [29] that advocates self-improvement and self-control. The idea to coin this term came to me after attending a management course.

---

[29] http://en.wikipedia.org/wiki/Stoicism

Expertise-Driven Motivation

There are many X-Driven motivations out there, but I prefer expertise-driven individuals, motivated by the desire to become experts. It is not bullshit, as you might think. It is more like a persistent psychological state found in researchers and scientists, and the best results are guaranteed when a money-driven positive feedback loop supplements it. I've seen such people in both software engineering and software technical support environments.

www.ingramcontent.com/pod-product-compliance
Lightning Source LLC
Chambersburg PA
CBHW050816090426
42736CB00022B/3476